Decorating
Your
Garden

Decorating Your Garden

Inspired Ways
to Use Ornamental
Objects and
Furnishings
Outdoors

Pat Ross

TIME®
LIFE
BOOKS

Time–Life Books, Alexandria, VA

Time-Life Books is a division of Time-Life, Inc.
President & CEO: George Artandi

Time-Life Books
President: Stephen Frary

Time-Life Custom Publishing
Vice President & Publisher: Terry Newell
Vice President of Sales & Marketing: Neil Levin
Director of Special Sales: Liz Ziehl
Director of Design: Christopher M. Register
Project Manager: Jennifer M. Lee
Production Manager: Carolyn Clark
Quality Assurance Manager: James D. King

Book Design: Howard Klein

First Printing. Printed in the U.S.A.

Time-Life is a trademark of Time Warner Inc. U.S.A.

Library of Congress Cataloging-in-Publication Data
Ross, Pat, 1943-
Decorating Your Garden: Inspired Ways to Use Ornamental Objects and Furnishings
Outdoors/Pat Ross
p.cm.
ISBN: 0-7835-5311-0
1. Garden ornaments and furniture. I. Title.
SB473.5.R65   1998   98-3820
717—dc21   CIP

Books produced by Time-Life Custom Publishing are available at special bulk discount for promotional and premium use. Custom adaptations can also be created to meet your specific marketing goals. Call (800) 323-5255.

For Ken
with love

CONTENTS

INTRODUCTION

THE PERSONALITY OF
THE GARDEN

As a child, at our home in rural

Maryland, I loved to play in the

great shiny leaves that bordered

our lawn, an expanse of cultivated

ground separated by a picket fence

from the fields beyond. At age

six, I preferred wild terrain to

manicured landscape, any day,

and got my comeuppance from

nature with a record-setting case

of poison ivy that I will never forget.

Many of this garden's worldly treasures, the decorative
objects and captivating ornamentation, are so skillfully inter-
woven with nature that, at first glance, they appear almost
hidden from view among the blooms and plantings.

Just last year, I wound up with a bright rash from trimming back the potted geraniums, the leaves and juice of which I now avoid. When Rufus meows and rubs up against me after prowling through the weeds, I begin to itch. Because of my background as a writer of interior design books, I suppose it is not surprising that I prefer to decorate gardens rather than plant in them—planning, acquiring, enjoying, and, of course, taking photographs, which involves great joy and little risk. This is my sublimated way of gardening, one that has frequently put me into other people's gardens with my camera and my admiration. Perhaps it's also because of my background that I turned to exterior design, or bringing the indoors outdoors with decorative accessories that add balance, charm, surprise, and satisfy.

I didn't set out to compile an encyclopedia on garden ornamentation. Instead, I sought to photograph and write about home gardens that had been enlivened with touches that reflect the personality and style of the garden owners. I never expected to discover such variety, creativity, and zeal. Gardeners are, of course, an obsessed group; doing battle with Bambi and the gang; going broke on mulch alone, yet shaping and cherishing plots ranging in size from postage-stamp backyards to grand estates. Decorating a garden gives people an opportunity to garden in yet another way; they partner with nature and, according to one gardener, "find objects to embellish natural ambiance and fill the soul." Many gardeners think that a garden is not complete without ornamentation. Their gardens are

ABOVE: This long-necked urn survived the trip from Paraguay to South Carolina, only to fall some years later in transit to the owners' garden in Virginia. To make the best of it, Elizabeth and Bruce Campbell created this clever spectacle in their garden. Mulching all around has helped the objects to stand out.

RIGHT: "We probably robbed a grave site!" declares the gardener facetiously about this devotional piece, purchased in the south of France. A mirror reflecting the statue and the summer garden is framed by trelliswork to create a meditative garden alcove. Because a mirror is uncommon outdoors, especially to birds who see only an extension of garden and sky, the hanging basket is a thoughtful warning for the avian population.

an extension of their homes, an exterior complement to their interior style. They'll talk your ear off about why and how they do what they do as they walk your legs off on a tour over hill and dale. This is exactly what I looked for (and looked forward to) as I traveled and gathered material for this book.

The philosophies, approaches, and styles of the 35 gardeners whose gardens appear in *Decorating Your Garden* are joyfully limitless. There is no one description that fits all. One peace-seeking gardener doesn't think twice about dragging heavy twig furniture into a meditative woodland alcove. Another is addicted to finding quirky pieces at cheap roadside stands. Many gardeners find catalogs offering "new garden toys" irresistible, while the more patient ones wait years for just the right stone sculpture to turn up. What they share is a joy in the whole fulfilling and, occasionally, exasperating process.

"I am constantly finding little gifts for my

RIGHT: The garden owners inherited this birdbath with the property. They believe it hasn't been moved in 40 years. Because of its simplicity against a majestic background, it is a perfect example of "less is more."

wall, move some furniture around," says garden designer Margaret Burnett. "And my garden is much the same way." The excitement of decorating any garden invloves the constant motion it implies as gardeners create vignettes of humor and delight and have great fun in the process.

The collector at heart sees the many nooks and crannies of a garden as opportunities for display. The garden becomes a museum without walls. There's little need to crowd or squeeze, and so revered objects take on heightened status in the great outdoors: a folk-art weathervane crowning a garden shed; a bronze lion, signed and dated, standing guard over a stone terrace; a primitive buggy bench picked up at a country auction, symbolizing rural traditions.

Other gardeners give new meaning to "How does your garden grow?" They have an eye for whimsical found objects and truly one-of-a-kind pieces discovered at tag sales, swap meets, and at

The branches of two great trees—an oak and a maple—have intertwined on this expansive stretch of lawn, which gives the adjacent gardens breathing room. An around-the-tree seat at the far end of the lawn provides a place to sit and ponder, possibly about mowing so much grass.

the frequently visited town dump. According to one gardener: "Everything has more than one life. If it stood before, you can lay it down, hang it, bury part of it, nail it to something, alter it, paint it. Look at all the money you'll save, not to mention being known as clever."

There's refuge in these created spaces. Sun-bleached wooden chairs in Betty Sherrill's "secret garden" on Long Island offer a place to pause for a cool drink before another round of weeding. Wind chimes provide the music. Tranquillity beckons from a shady bench by the goldfish pond, a solitary hammock among the roses on a sultry day, or a full-length mirror that appears to multiply the peonies in bloom during an evening stroll. Many gardeners leave their watches indoors and use a sundial, a thoughtful, if rarely exact, reminder of ancient astronomy and our never-ending connection with the

A serene blanket of winter snow shows clearly the structure or "bones" of any garden. Devoid of color, the various forms in this uncluttered tableau of objects, furniture, structures, and bold plantings invite closer inspection.

heavens. There is entertainment value, too, in a decorated garden. Weddings, parties, tea for two, or wine before dinner are more comfortable and inviting when celebrated outdoors.

"When creatures come to your garden, you've mastered gardening," declares Barbara Pressler, who creates habitats for birds, butterflies, and other animals in her rural Pennsylvania garden. She provides birdbaths, wind and water features, and plenty of feeders. In gardens everywhere, plaques honoring Noah and statues of Saint Francis pay homage in ways that enhance and embellish.

Objects and ornamentation have a different value under the sun, in the shadow of the moon, and during a good rain. I found this out as I photographed gardens in six states in all kinds of weather. In the state of Washington, an umbrella became essential equipment when it rained nine days straight. The garden worlds then took on a solemn wet look, stone and metal slick and gleaming. Little pops of light on otherwise hazy days gave the flowers a special richness. Orbs, statues, urns, lawn chairs were all shellacked by nature. Moments before a torrential downpour, Diane Glenn's lakeside garden filled with a heavenly glow as lightning cracked and the sky darkened in the distance. During a New England heat wave, the sun bleached both the gardens and me flat and pale by 9:00 a.m., but sunrise provided a halo of splendid light so thin and clear that the mood of objects was changed entirely. Sometimes the long shadows cast by a statue or an urn mean twice the satisfaction. The glow of sunset creates a radiance that washes over entire gardens, giving them the warmth of good country butter. Thick mountain mist and creeping seaside fog shroud garden objects in an eerie veil until the sun sets them free. Moonlight works its own wonders by creating bold and magical silhouettes.

The shifting seasons add to this ever-changing tableau. During times of growth, garden adornment blends with the plantings. In the fall, the role begins to shift as objects stand out among the harvest colors and fading foliage. Winter brings a spareness that magnifies a garden's shapes and forms. Under the cover of a new snowfall, the human-made structure of the garden is most easily admired. Every season is the right season for garden decoration.

My notebook is filled with notes, words of wisdom from the gardeners who know best. I find that I've jotted down: "Everything in life flows, and never does it flow more freely than in the presence of nature." Other words are circled: "I think of my garden as my home, and I live in my home." Then I find the most reassuring quote of all scribbled in a margin: "It will all work out." When all is said and done, objects provide a sense of permanence to a constantly changing scene. They show the world that you have truly moved in and plan to stay. Eventually, the personality of a gardener extends beyond garden spaces, spilling over gates and fences into the hearts of everyone who passes by. Perhaps it's this spirited and contagious energy of the decorated garden that I find most appealing of all.

REFLECTING THE ELEMENTS

A birdbath fills with rainwater and becomes the local watering hole. The gentle trickle of a fountain lends tranquillity. Wind chimes send a musical announcement of the shifting breezes. A shadow cast on the face of a sundial reminds us of our precious time in the garden. The significance and beauty of many garden objects is magnified when they harmonize with water, wind, and sunlight.

LEFT: A color-washed concrete pool, designed to mimic a morning glory and filled with lilies, mixes naturally with shrubs and perennials and serves as a counterpoint to seasonal shifts in color.

"I enjoy the small dramas," mentions David Lewis, as I set up my camera in his Washington State garden. He is referring to a small pool in which delicate miniature lilies float on top. They unfold every afternoon at approximately the same time and close shortly thereafter. Luckily, I am there for what soon feels like opening night. "The lilies are a gift, one of nature's windows of opportunity," he adds. Soon the drama begins and the lilies burst open, providing me with a welcomed photo opportunity.

Many other water features—fountains, basins, and whimsical reservoirs—are as much for the frolicking of garden creatures as they are for the pleasure of human visitors. Shimmering mirrors reflecting the sky ripple and spill over their boundaries, dripping rhythmically. A bird feather and an autumn leaf float like little boats. Seeds sprout and are quickly snatched by passing birds.

Moisture is a friendly place to grow thick, green moss. Gardeners impatient for a covering of

Virginia gardener Elizabeth Campbell held the winning number to a most extraordinary door prize at a local garden show. Over time, the birdbath has developed a pleasing patina, blending with the antique objects in her predominantly formal garden.

nature's velvet recommend coating a garden object with buttermilk, then placing it in a shady spot. Over time, the moss grows lush and bright.

A Long Island gardener living near the sea found a way to keep her backyard creatures happy through the long, harsh winter months. She salvaged the top of a large stone birdbath and set it on a pallet of branches. When the temperature drops, she places two 40-watt bulbs underneath to keep the birdbath from becoming a skating rink, with extension cords hidden in the thick pachysandra. This wildlife spa attracts all kinds of birds, from wrens to seagulls, with neighborhood squirrels and a few ducks splashing during off-hours.

Sundials are an ancient mystery, their voices speaking from antiquity. Their designs range from a simple vertical dial on a wall to an elaborate armillary whose airy metal rings represent the circles of the celestial sphere. In one herb garden,

"My cat and the late afternoon birds share this little oasis," says the owner of this bit of garden whimsy, adding, "I'm sure the neighborhood raccoons also stop by to wash down some of the goldfish in my pond."

a sundial sits high on a classical pillar above a pretty cover of lavender, serving as a focal point for this celestial-themed garden. Another gardener has lined a walkway with a treasured collection of sundials, adding architecture and dignity.

Birdbaths, fountains, and sundials share centuries-old origins. The chosen style is a matter of taste. An ornate piece might be a Gothic antique that dominates the lawn or one with a more abstract, contemporary design. The eclectic range of styles could make even the most serious collector dizzy.

"Our garden is such an extension of our home that it's not only the sights that please us from a doorway or window, but also the sounds," says a Connecticut gardener. "The birds splashing, the water trickling, the tiny bells making a racket in a strong breeze . . . . When our windows are thrown open in the summer, we're lulled to sleep by the garden music."

ABOVE: A contemporary rendition of a square birdbath shows strength in simplicity. Garden artists George Little and David Lewis of Bainbridge Island, Washington, created this dynamic water feature.

LEFT: The garden owners who discovered this cast cement and mica birdbath at an antiques shop were charmed by its unusual square shape. They placed it under a sheltering tree, where it has been able to develop an emerald green moss.

RIGHT: Fine garden objects are often left behind when property changes hands. The new owners of this substantial birdbath were thrilled to inherit it. It anchors a woodsy area of the garden near the property line.

ABOVE: On a brilliant fall day, a simple concrete birdbath stands out amid fading hosta, pyracantha, and daylilies. As winter sets in, the birdbath is valued for the form it brings to the bare scene.

RIGHT: This whimsical grouping of lotus-leaf birdbaths is made of color-washed concrete. "We liked the playfulness of the five together," say the owners. Indeed, the birdbaths appear to be planted in the garden among the silver morning-glories, hosta, and the long, pointed leaves of bugloss.

LEFT: A Pompeian putto peeks out from a cover of trailing begonia and violets. The classical winged cherubic infant is but one of many little surprises in a garden where an abundance of terra-cotta objects gives the overall garden an earthy connection.

RIGHT: This raven-decorated pedestal is also a fountain, adding height to a spot in the garden and the pleasurable drift of trickling water.

BELOW: Mary Beth and Jerry Satterlee were inspired to design their own courtyard fountain after a trip to Italy, where they strolled along narrow stone streets and noticed charming small fountains in wall niches at every turn. Placing a coyote-shaped fountain spout on an ivy-covered wall, they later discovered just the right timeworn pot to serve as the basin.

RIGHT: The mood is mischievous as two lead frogs spit long-distance into the garden below. The imaginative placement of the frog fountains has turned this garden scene into a whimsical drama.

LEFT: This wistful little statue of Pan had been banished to the trash pile at the local garden center because the head had broken off. "Nothing a little silicon epoxy couldn't fix," says the gardener who rescued him and built a water garden. She lined the pool with plastic and edged it with rounded rocks. Mossy creeping speedwell blooms blue in summer and turns bronze in fall.

RIGHT: With his feet under the lily pads hiding the pond's pump below, this garden sculpture of an otter looks as if he just popped out of the water to take a look at the tranquil scene around him.

ABOVE: Old Japanese fishing-net floats washed ashore on many beaches in Washington State between the 1920s and the 1960s. Made of blown glass, they were wrapped in the knotted rope that had attached them to the nets. These glass floats reflect the light in the garden under a blinding midday sun.

LEFT: This copper fish sculpture by Milton Williams, an artist from Carmel, California, floats reflected in the pond's still water.

Digital watches and computerized alarm clocks haven't diminished our fascination with the ancient sundial as a timepiece and an architectural form. If ancient Stonehenge was a sundial, then it's safe to say that the sundial has the longest history of all garden objects, the earliest identified sundials having been developed in ancient Egypt and Mesopotamia. Created in brass, slate, lead, cast iron, and stone, the sundial's beautifully crafted designs can range from plain to ornate. The organic way they work registering the shadow cast by the sun as it makes its diurnal path across the sky has long fascinated us, feeding our romantic attachment to them. The renowned English garden designer Gertrude Jekyll declared at the turn of the century, "A sundial is always welcome in pleasure ground."

Here, a handsome bronze armillary represents the sundial's lyrical form at its finest. It sits unadorned as the focal point in a wide stretch of lawn. The gardener has selected a classical base with details and proportions to harmonize with and balance the object.

The Good-Woman Scarecrow

"You can't keep a good woman down" is the message of this thoroughly nontraditional scarecrow created by gardener Barbara Pressler for a garden in western Pennsylvania.

The body structure of the strong farm woman was made from leftover, odd-sized wood scraps tossed out by a local ladder company. They were screwed together so that the arms and legs are movable. The stockings are a pair of thick men's cotton socks cuffed at the ankles. Curlers and a synthetic wig sit upon her environmentally correct birdhouse head. (For a different type of head, an armature made of chicken wire can be filled with sphagnum.) A large apron with pockets holds several safety pins for emergencies. According to Barbara, "My grandmother and her friends always wore safety pins on their aprons and clothes almost like jewelry." Naturally, this sensible woman trudges through the garden in well-worn Red Cross shoes. A healthy bosom and fanny, made up of many plastic bags, round her out. Barbara Pressler stuffed her plastic bags with leaves, keeping the body form light. She suggests that plastic peanuts would work as well.

PRECEDING PAGES: A souvenir bell from Disney World hangs quietly in a crabapple tree that will bloom white in spring, followed by small red fruit. When a brisk wind comes along, the petite bell sings out a delicate chime.

LEFT: Set on a simple stone pedestal and placed in a gloriously unruly part of the garden, an early-twentieth-century sundial provides a needed focal point before the garden blends into woodland beyond.

RIGHT: Graceful wind ornaments made of copper bob in the breeze, reflecting the light and catching the attention of birds and butterflies. The metal hummingbirds were created by artisan Milton Williams.

CLASSICAL ORNAMENTATION

Formal ornamentation keeps company with boxwood and roses and reminds us of a romantic past. From the grandest garden to the most pocket-sized, time-honored pieces lend elegance, grace, and a sense of antiquity. An enchanting stone maiden brings serenity to a courtyard; two menacing lead griffins stand vigil; a winsome cherub lolls on the lawn.

LEFT: One of four ominous-looking bird figures adorn the base of an impressive lead fountain.

RIGHT: This enchanting figure is symbolic of summer's blooming. Placed between a bed of ample peonies and a thick expanse of ivy that has spread all the way to the property line, the statue accentuates the division in this romantic Victorian garden and sets the period tone.

Taming the Wildness Beyond

The land behind Tommie and Robert Duke's Virginia home changes from manicured lawn to untamed overgrowth as the rolling hillside sweeps abruptly into the woods. This topography provided the perfect opportunity to terrace sections of the hill for garden entertaining. Being from New Orleans, Tommie felt at home with classical architecture and knew that she wanted a formal balustrade for structure on the lowest level of the property. With their daughter's garden wedding barely a year away, a plan was under way.

"Only the concept was easy," Tommie explained as she recalled her frustration. "Finding the perfect balusters was impossible." So the couple decided to create them. Bob

Duke worked with a local carpenter designing the molds; then the balusters and railings were cast in cement. After that, the ornamentation seemed almost effortless.

Cast-stone statues of the four seasons from a shop in New Orleans' French Quarter were placed in pairs at either end of the wall, flanking large urns and creating a

scene from antiquity. Spring carries an armload of blooms; Summer brings a bounty of grapes; Autumn offers sheaves of wheat, while chilly Winter bundles up against the cold. The backdrop of dense woodland beyond stands in unusual contrast to this dramatic scene.

They finished the terrace just in time for their daughter's lovely June wedding.

An excellent bronze reproduction of a Victorian devotional piece, possibly funerary in origin, this angel from England occupies a contemplative spot, separated from the upper part of a terraced garden by boxwood that provides unfailing greenery throughout the fall and winter months. The boxwood alcove existed long before the owners decided to create a focal point there with the sculpture. Perennial borders add fullness and color during blooming seasons. "In England, it's what they like to call herbacious borders," the Anglophile owners add.

LEFT: Most gardeners prefer the look of brand-new garden objects after they've weathered a bit. Settled in the shade of a cherry tree among wild mint, this cherub is beginning to show the pleasing signs of age.

RIGHT: Hebe, the daughter of Zeus, graciously presides at the end of a brick path bordered by boxwood. Her alabaster form stands out against the dense, verdant background.

LEFT: Balanced on a hill of rocks in the distance, an engaging angel looks over this serene gathering spot. In the foreground, 20-foot lengths of rebar found at a farm sale make an unusual arched pergola on which flowering vines climb, wind, and bloom.

RIGHT: This devotional figure adds a sense of quiet contemplation to an alcove in a large garden where levels were created by stone walls and winding paths. The angel, while modest in size, has been mounted on a stone pedestal to provide height and focus to a low area.

FOLLOWING PAGES, LEFT: Staddle stones once supported the foundations of ancient granaries. Their curious toadstool shapes prevented vermin from reaching the stores. Some of these stones date back more than 500 years, though most are from the eighteenth century. Even though they are expensive and hard to find, they make fascinating garden ornaments, lining a driveway or forming a focal point. Joni Nelson prizes the one fine English staddle stone in her Long Island garden.

FOLLOWING PAGES, RIGHT: A terra-cotta shelf nailed to a sheltering apple tree can hold small pots of shade-loving impatiens or pansies for color. Or it can simply serve as decoration, perhaps catching the attention of passersby.

ABOVE: An unusual nineteenth-century trio of stone toadstools serves as the perfect foreground accent for a border of sedum, 'Stella de Oro' daylilies, and artemisia, giving it a storybook charm.

RIGHT: The garden owners bought this new stone snail its "Made in Mexico" label still attached, because its whimsical yet refined form appealed to them. Hoping to speed up the slow aging process and make their snail look as though it had been around for a long time, they rubbed buttermilk on its surface, then set it in the shade to encourage the development of moss. In this case, the popular buttermilk treatment worked wonders, making the new snail look well established.

LEFT: A boxwood topiary and soft mounds of lemon thyme have been planted to mimic the rush and ripple of water in the basin of an impressive antique iron fountain guarded by great birds. With these plantings, a traditional garden piece is given a clever spin and an inspired new use.

BELOW: It's a long drip to the ground from the planted capitals of contemporary concrete columns that were designed as classically inspired water features. Their imposing forms establish a rather grand sense of antiquity while at the same time lulling the soul with their constant water music.

LEFT: This heavy lead urn was shipped home from the south of France. The owner confesses that it cost so much to ship the urns that she "just didn't want to spend any more to fix them up!" In truth, the lovely natural finish is perfect.

RIGHT: Poised for many years on the grounds of an east coast Victorian mansion, this rare cast-iron griffin, manufactured circa 1870, is one of a pair that traveled from an auction in Maine to a house in Seattle. The formidable pair guards the entrance, surrounded by a riot of summer plantings, including an exotic banana plant, geraniums, and clematis.

BELOW: Ivy cascades over the rim of a classical stone urn set on an iron pedestal. It centers this meditative shade garden.

This serene tableau can change from a dramatic silhouette at daybreak, as seen on the opposite page, to a dazzling portrait at noon, seen in the photograph above. On a rainy day, the elegant pair of bronze herons glistens and shines; sunset brings a golden glow to the figures, which are set around a mossy stone-lined pond filled with frogs and sunfish.

Gardeners are keen observers of light, constantly aware of the way the presence or absence of it can totally alter the appearance of flowers and objects alike. One gardener commented that it's almost like watching scenes in a revolving play, light being the great director. Spotlights on selected features in the garden further enhance the small evening dramas.

RIGHT: It was a challenge for Mary Beth Satterlee to lug this iron obelisk home by plane to Seattle after she'd retrieved it from a friend's junk pile. This rags-to-riches story ends happily with the obelisk standing out in a crowd of Japanese anemones in the Satterlees' front yard.

ABOVE: "I love to resurrect the best of old cottage gardens," says one gardener, "so I placed a gazing ball in the shaded corner of our courtyard border to reflect the garden in front of it, the cherry tree branches above it, and the faces of all the friends who seek their smiles there."

RIGHT: Victorian gazing balls are available in a range of colors and add a gleam of light to spots in the garden. This blue gazing ball is a reproduction of a giant Christmas ball. The gardeners also own a silver one, and they interchange the balls depending on the season and what's in bloom. The different seasonal light affects the color and mood of any gazing ball; silver is particularly effective in winter, when it reflects the snow. However, high winds can wreak havoc on such fragile objects, which is why this one has been placed in a sheltered area.

FAR RIGHT: This silver gazing globe reflects the house and the foliage around it like a curious fun-house mirror.

Garden sheds and basement alcoves are filled with a mind-boggling variety of containers that gardeners collect, even hoard, for use outdoors. Garden shops stack them to the sky: urns, pots, planters, vases, jardinieres, tanks, troughs, and tubs. Many containers display classical motifs that date back to the vessels of antiquity. Others are as familiar as the well-loved terra-cotta flowerpot.

Karen and Pope Woodard have lifted container gardening to an art form in their spacious Virginia garden. They use containers to better establish seating areas, to suggest borders, accent paths and walkways, edge plantings, and to announce an entranceway. Containers to help create a focal point or add a burst of color. And everyone can see the blooms when vessels sit high on pedestals or are just placed on empty pots that have been turned upside down.

The Woodards prefer simple terra cotta because it allows the color and texture of the

This antique-looking urn, overflowing with asparagus fern and decorated with a classical grape motif, is actually rather new.

flowers to make a lasting impression. Karen and Pope have a penchant for collecting small objects: seashells and stones from the beach nearby; glass shards; and miniature figurines that they display around the potted plants.

"Containers are our moveable feast," says Karen. "We can create a whole new architecture just by transferring pots of flowers and herbs from one place to another." With an assortment of shapes and sizes close at hand, gardeners are assured of having a container just the right size and scale for spot dress-up. Also, with this moveable feast comes the ability to enjoy the flowers and the lasting greenery long after the first frost has chased us from the garden. There are ledges and window sills waiting for the still-flourishing geraniums and potted herbs that can sit usefully on a kitchen window sill till spring.

Many gardeners believe "the pot's the thing." They'll display containers alone as decorative objects—their softly curving forms and earthy colors making dramatic statements. One garden owner refused to pay one penny more to repair an expensive urn whose neck had chipped noticeably during an just as expensive long-distance trip. So she set the handsome, though damaged, urn on the ground topsy-turvy next to its intended pedestal, creating a witty little scenario for her garden.

I've always been attracted to the benefits of this type of confined gardening, especially since poison ivy rarely creeps into the pots. Containers allow for impulse: move it, change it, rearrange it. It's what many of us do with our bookcases and our closets in the house on rainy days. I thought about the merits of containers as I photographed the design of a southwestern vessel with my closeup lens. When I moved on to an even tighter shot of exquisite laurel-wreath handles on a French urn, I grasped the aesthetic satisfaction that such container objects have brought to gardeners for centuries.

An ornate planter filled with scavola has been set atop an antique English plinth.

PRECEDING PAGES: An old whiskey barrel seemed the perfect container for a lovely rare dwarf green laceleaf Japanese maple, which was being decimated by the local deer population. By placing the planter near a stone wall close to the house, where deer are not so brazen, the thriving maple tree fills a corner with color and texture.

ABOVE: A mossy terra-cotta pot planted with strap cactus and maidenhair fern has been elevated on a small stand in the hothouse.

RIGHT: In the 1940s and the 1950s, folk artists created containers and benches from composition material, such as cement, to resemble stumps, branches, and even mushrooms. Hidden among growing things, thetree stump looks natural in the garden.

An Earthly Container

Here is a recipe passed along by gardener Diane Glenn of Seattle. "This container was made about forty years ago by my mother, Rachel Stetchfield. She's now eighty-nine, still gardening and playing bridge and very sharp. I called her for the recipe." Nestled in the earth and seen in the photograph at left, Diane's container is filled with lewisia.

3 parts sand

1 part cement

1 part perlite or peat moss

Combine all ingredients. Add water until the mixture is the consistency of brown sugar. Shape over a mound of dirt or form inside a container, such as a plastic washbasin. Make a hole in the bottom for drainage.

Playful rosettes of stone add to the enormous charm of this pebble planter, purchased by Ingrid Savage during a California "road trip" with her friend and business partner, Diane Glenn. Their *Hat & The Heart* business specializes in handcrafted objects. Although the two women are always on the lookout for unusual pieces in unlikely places for clients, they admit that pieces as irresistible as this one might wind up on their own doorstep. Over the years, Diane and Ingrid have found that crafts shows, local artisans, and small shops and galleries in out-of-the-way locations can be fabulous places to find handcrafted treasures that you won't see in your neighbor's garden. They'll frequently pull off the main road to follow handmade signs, as well as their own well-honed instincts.

LEFT: You can enjoy a strawberry pot first for the bloom and then for the reward.

ABOVE: A simple pot containing a colorful bromeliad has settled into its surroundings as though it had been planted in the ground. Using large potted plants in a garden allows for arrangements to be changed on a creative whim.

LEFT: A birdbath richly encrusted with pebbles is filled with a variety of thyme. This was a find from a roadside sculpture stand in California. According to the gardener, "Most of the merchandise at the roadside stand was yes, you guessed it, tacky! But I loved these handcrafted pieces, which were dirt cheap. And so I bought two."

TOP RIGHT: Patches of characteristic green and gold paint endure on a vintage toy replica of a John Deere wagon. Phipps, a cairn terrier, stands guard over the wagon's cargo, a flat of pachysandra.

BOTTOM RIGHT: A venerable potted rosemary fits well into the seat opening of an old-fashioned "throne." Faddi, the cat, has found shelter there.

ABOVE AND RIGHT: Grand-scale objects were sought to establish access along a lengthy brick path, one step down, that leads to the distant part of the garden. When this pair of classical iron containers turned up, the owners planted them with Alberta spruce for a torchlike appearance, providing architectural shape to this area. The bold figures of griffins around the base of the four-foot containers are familiar to classical adornment.

LEFT: The rustic design of these square pots planted with cheerful begonias suits this Connecticut stone wall perfectly.

ABOVE: A small English trough planted with miniature herbs and
sedum sits on a wooden bench for up-close viewing.

ABOVE: Sedum spills over the top of a distressed concrete garden pillar. Columns in varying heights and diameters can provide a focal point and vertical accent in an area of the garden needing definition.

ABOVE: The alyssum cascading from the pockets of this aged strawberry pot were planted from seed.

RIGHT: A concrete curb was the only break between the narrow parking area and a rolling lawn before the homeowners beautified this unbecoming division with soft plantings and pots of bright flowers. The Adirondack table and chairs, described as "our moving patio," migrate from place to place as different areas of the garden are at their peak beauty.

ABOVE: The dark and brilliant glaze of a Berber cooking pot from southern Morocco, roped with copper ivy, takes on an added dimension as sunlight filters through a sheltered part of the garden.

LEFT: The witty handling of two Mediterranean-style vessels half-hidden by a tall sheaf of metallic blue switch grass introduces an element of fun.

ABOVE: Two handcrafted vessels, carefully carted home to a Virginia garden
from a vacation in Paraguay, have been kept together in a rock-filled part of
the garden.

LEFT: The friendly proportions of this antique water jar, combined with a
green glaze, the color of summer's most verdant foliage, make it the perfect
candidate to stand out in a crowd among the traditional planted vessels.

AT HOME IN THE GARDEN

Garden spaces are simply rooms without walls, places where interior design moves outdoors. It's as easy as dragging a comfortable chair and a good book to the pond's edge or as ambitious as designing a table made of shards that seats eight. Gardeners are an imaginative lot, and they work tirelessly to create gratifying extensions of their homes that reflect not only their lifestyles but their personalities as well.

After a day of energetic weeding, Fred and Marcie Imberman look forward to heading for this idyllic spot above "Lake Fred," where they rest their weary bones on comfortable Adirondack chairs.

A breezy porch that cries out for a swing, a wooden deck with cheerful geraniums, a stone terrace that moves our lives closer to nature—such spaces are wonderful empty outdoor rooms waiting to be furnished. There are also private nooks and crannies, stretches of lawn, and secret gardens given to solitary moments. Size is never a factor. From a small walled garden to a rolling lawn, natural surroundings become comfortable and inviting places for just one or even for a crowd when typical outdoor pieces are effectively paired with more domestic styles.

Mirrors are magical. They magnify a scattering

The just ahead "Lake Fred" sign was a gift from a close friend who drove 130 miles just to celebrate the "opening" of Marcie and Fred Imberman's Connecticut pond in the small meadow behind their country home.

of lilies or allow a reflective view of a hidden garden statue. Coffee tables are essential props for everything from the Sunday paper to weary feet. A hammock in a cool spot can become a well-deserved vacation. Some people require that a chair or settee be as comfortable as their beloved easy chairs; others are willing to put up with a less yielding iron seat for the pleasure of its decorative beauty.

"I see my whole garden as an opportunity to go shopping," admits a garden owner who says she's queen of the garden catalogs. She shops by mail and she shops till she drops. "I'm hooked on the whole process of placing, replacing, fixing up, and even changing things around." Since any garden exists in a constant state of flux, decorating outdoors is much like getting new wallpaper every season under a pale blue ceiling.

Primitive pieces that withstand the elements well, such as old tables and buggy seats, are still found at country auctions and tag sales. Of course, the decorative garden furniture that truly endures are the iron and stone pieces that grow more important with age. There are new handcrafted collectibles as well as sculptured stone furniture and whimsical twig pieces to provide an unusual touch.

"Please make yourself at home," Don Haynie told me as he dashed off to the airport; and so I took him at his word. With my camera set up, I waited patiently for that rosy light that comes just before sunset. "Home" was the expansive herb garden at Buffalo Springs Herb Farm in western Virginia, which he and Tom Hamlin own. There was time to spare, so my companion drove to the nearby village to pick up something to eat. He returned with a wedge of cheese, a long loaf of French bread, and a bottle of chilled white wine, complete with two rather elegant stemmed glasses in nonbreakable plastic. We set up our little party on a round country table sheltered by a shady trellised alcove. "What a job!" I quipped as I took advantage of the evening's radiant glow and a memorable sunset in my host's well-appointed garden.

This winsome plaster man in the moon provided the perfect storybook ending for a deep scar in a favorite cherry tree where a diseased limb was removed. Now it's easy to find this country house by the handcrafted number or by the light of the moon.

ABOVE: Ancient Greek temple ruins inspired the design of this commanding Sounion table and stools that make their own timeless statement. Impervious to the elements, the natural stone anchors a garden landscape about to shift into its fall colors.

RIGHT: An inviting spot near the house becomes a summer room for two.

ABOVE: A typical northwest downpour has left a rich sheen of moisture on the many shade plants in the backyard refuge of Brian Coleman's Victorian home where two large terra-cotta balls, originally used as decorative ornaments for a late-nineteenth-century building, rest near a mid-nineteenth-century Gothic wrought-iron bench. The owner has taken great care to furnish his garden exclusively with original period pieces.

LEFT: The owner deliberately left the wrought iron unpainted to give it a weathered air of summers past. The detail is Eastlake with Gothic touches, a mixture of styles typically Victorian.

Our Victorian ancestors, who adored fancy wicker and ornate iron furniture, extended those same passions to the rococo swirls and flourishes of garden furniture created with strong steel wire. Their greenhouses and gardens became treasure troves of this relatively lightweight, portable, and romantic furniture that bragged of accessories galore. From filigree tables and mesh chair to whimsical bird cages and hanging baskets, one piece seemed to top the next in its extravagant degree of ornamentation. Over the years, the understandably fragile nature of the wire has made it more more difficult to find period pieces in fine condition.

That's why the delicate late nineteenth-century wire garden chair is such a treat for its form as well as its function. The owners left the chair in its original condition and place it under a Japanese maple. Meanwhile, a bright green hops vine has extended its reach to the chair, seen in the detail at the right.

Inspired by historical references, many of today's designers have turned their attention to developing distinctive and charming garden furniture in wire, stoking an old flame.

ABOVE: A matched pair of superb ornate cast-iron chairs done in a popular fern design and dating from about 1875 stands out against the reassuring simplicity of a traditional New England country home.

LEFT: A Gothic influence can be seen in this cast-iron garden seat with its segmented back and restrained pierced design. Placed in the shade near a rambling stone wall, the piece stands out against the gray stonework.

LEFT: Elana Korakianitou, an artist whose work has appeared in major galleries and museums around the country, has created this table for her own Seattle courtyard from found ceramic and metal objects, seen in detail in the smaller photograph. Paired with striking black garden furniture, the sheltered area has become the perfect place for outdoor entertaining.

BELOW: A set of dainty iron furniture adds interest to the space near an old brick wall where ivy garlands have been trained to cascade over the sides. Many gardeners say they are drawn to these petite sets because they fool the eye into seeing a larger lawn or because they make a confined area appear grand.

LEFT: Painted white, then black, this iron garden bench has a changing history. The black is gradually being washed away by the rain, leaving an unusual mottled finish that nature has had a good hand in creating.

Many antique iron pieces have been painted and repainted many times over. However, it's possible to have iron furniture professionally sandblasted, or steel brushed and sandpapered. The fresh paint can then be applied over the natural finish. And iron furniture stripped to its original, unprotected state has recently found favor inside the house as an accent piece. However, most collectors simply consider the irregularities part of the charm.

ABOVE: Betty Sherrill will never run out of her trademark garden hats, from baseball caps to the more typical straw styles, having accumulated a seemingly countless collection from her frequent travels. They hang on hat-racks in the hallways of her Long Island home, and often wind up on this rustic iron-frame bench, with its wooden slatted seat and back.

RIGHT: A sturdy steel-framed bench such as this evokes fond memories of public parks and Sunday picnics. The owners repainted their garden icon a color they love: deep forest green.

ABOVE: The sculptural qualities of the massive slab bench by Seattle artist Brian Goldbloom called for an uncluttered natural setting where the bench could be both used and admired.

LEFT: When friends delivered the 500-pound slab of slate in the back of their truck to Barbara Pressler as a garden surprise, asking, "Okay, where do you want us to put it?," Barbara promptly located two perfect rocks to use as a base for her immovable object. The slate was soon identified as an old curb used for lateral parking in one of the nearby farm towns. The indentation allowed a drainage pipe to spill onto the street. Now a permanent garden fixture, a profusion of gold sedge has given the bench a breezy sense of leisure.

ABOVE: Teak was the wood of choice for this exposed bench and trellis because it weathers softly and holds up over time. In the summertime, the grapevines provide a shady spot under which to sit and look out on the lower part of the garden.

LEFT: An avid gardener looks forward to lunchtime, when she can sit quietly in her "secret garden." "That's where I have my sandwiches," she says with enormous pleasure.

LEFT: A lovely old mirror in need of resilvering and a bit of new plaster has been nestled among fern, penstemon, and day lilies, facing away from direct sunlight and then tilted to reflect two other gardens. No matter where you look, there's a garden.

RIGHT AND FAR RIGHT: "This is my living room outdoors," says this garden owner. A mirror painted cranberry red that hangs on the patio wall was an auction find. "I played with it till every angle held a picture," says the gardener. With the addition of six ornate hat hooks for garden gloves and hats, the mirror is protected by the roof's overhang, expanding the definition of home decorating.

FOLLOWING PAGES, LEFT: A wall mirror bearing the image of the Greek king Oedipus breaks a long stretch of functional yard fencing and reflects a sea of rain-slicked ivy all around.

FOLLOWING PAGES, RIGHT: A jungle snake has invaded Eden, this time as part of a boldly colored concrete plaque. Its small silvery mirror provides a reverse peek at the garden for anyone who takes the time to discover this charming detail.

Please Read the Signs

Long before garden signs turned into a national pastime, with clever new logos and old sayings popping up like daisies, most signs were plain plaques of a purely functional nature: *Do not walk on the grass.* Along city streets, the stern admonitions ranged from *Curb your dog elsewhere* to *Do not pick the flowers.* We grew so accustomed to these signs that we simply looked the other way.

Luckily, we've entered a new age of sign consciousness. Memorable expressions about gardening are etched in stone as garden-style pet rocks have come into vogue.

Perhaps the most meaningful signs are the handmade ones, cheerful and inspired artwork that even the kids can get excited about. But in the words of one sign maven: "Now that people are bending to read every sign along the garden path, just be sure you spell all the words right."

THE
UNEXPECTED

"The imagination needs noodling—
long, inefficient, happy, idling,
dawdling and puttering."
—Brenda Ueland, 1938

The most valuable garden tool is a

gardener's lighthearted vision. The

idea of decorating a garden should

include spontaneity, whimsy, per-

sonal touches, and not too much

careful planning. Letting go of pre-

dictable notions means more room

for folly. Trusting your instincts

yields unexpected surprises and a

refreshing new take on gardening.

RIGHT: A discarded faceted glass doorknob has become
a garden treasure as it catches and refracts the late
afternoon sun. It sparkles next to Brazilian verbena, a tall
lavender biennial that attracts butterflies.

"I was born to break the rules," admits a maverick gardener as she finds the just-right spot on a craggy boulder for a splendid Victorian cut-glass doorknob she had saved from the local dump. It perfectly harmonizes with its new setting. "It reflects the wonderful light in this part of my rock garden," she points out.

A doorknob may be an extremely unusual garden object. But what makes this aesthetically pleasing found object so different from an iron obelisk or a reflective gazing ball? I soon found myself a joyful convert to the unexpected.

Countless gardeners are given to the placement of whimsical accessories, beloved souvenirs, and personal trinkets; in short, all the wonderful bric-a-brac that makes every garden one-of-a-kind. They believe that what counts is what amuses them and not what impresses anyone else. So instead of being quick to rush off to the garden center, these gardeners look around their

When the front garden met head-on with a sidewalk fire hydrant, the owners decided to dress up the hydrant. By doing so, they've created a colorful and unusual garden object.

own property for marvelous timeworn garden gates to hold up the drooping hydrangeas, a salvaged piece of decorative fencing to establish the perimeter of a new peony bed, or an odd rubber boot to hold tall yellow daisies. More traditional gardeners may find the devotees of tag sales and the saviors of almost-lost treasures somewhat bewildering. But there is actually a method to this madness and good lessons to be learned.

Whether it's therapeutic fun, recreation, or yet another expression of one's personality, there's much agreement about how unexpected garden objects work best. "I just keep walking around until I find the right place." You do have to be subtle about the placement of objects of any kind, from the classical and restrained to the unique and the outlandish. Some gardeners favor the "hide-and-seek" method of placing unexpected objects, making you think you have just stumbled onto them. Bold ornamentation, especially architectural remnants, requires a skillful weaving into the framework of a lawn or a planting bed. The rules regarding scale, texture, and color are also important when working with unusual objects to keep them from dominating the scene.

The personalized object comes in many forms. A tilework plaque displays a loving message to a lost friend; a concrete block that sparkles with bright shards is a gift from an artistic daughter; an iron star represents an interest in architectural and celestial history. And perhaps the most spontaneous objects are the handcrafted ones. Many gardeners are happiest when elbow deep in a tub of concrete and most satisfied when the birdhouses are of their own design. Shells, pottery shards, polished glass, and weathered barnboard are some of the inspiring raw materials that make these gardeners wax eloquently about the joys of gardening. The unexpected soon becomes expected pleasure.

A Deco-style gate from Singapore embellishes a garden filled with luxuriant hydrangeas. The gate needed steel footings that were welded by hand.

SHE DIGS IN HER GARDEN
WITH A SHOVEL AND A SPOON
SHE WEEDS HER LAZY LETTUCE
BY THE LIGHT OF THE MOON

ABOVE: A tribute to a lost friend who was an avid gardener, this mosaic plaque of small tiles is framed with old bricks. The verse was found among the friend's possessions, jotted on a scrap of paper and tucked in a book. The author of the verse remains a mystery.

LEFT: Reflecting the sun and glistening in the rain, this ever-changing amber-colored glass sphere is a fishing-net float used by Japanese fishermen.

FAR LEFT: A creative gardener glued some of her favorite shards to a bowling ball to make this home-built orb, then used dark blue grout to hold it together. It peeps out from amid 'Autumn Joy' stonecrop.

ABOVE: The bank sign provides the perfect display ledge for seashore treasures.

RIGHT: While it may seem unexpected, a cast-iron sign from a bank truly belongs in this Virginia garden. The garden owner's great-grandfather had been the bank's president as well as the original owner of the garden and its grand "beach cottage." When the sign was discovered in a warehouse in Norfolk, Virginia, the current owner snapped it up and installed the sign as a memorial of sorts. He planted his maternal grandmother's prize irises in front of the wall. The family enjoys dividing and sharing them each spring.

"All the Men in My Life"

That's how Pennsylvania gardener Barbara Pressler refers to the small bronze figures on these pages. She said they were sent to her by a friend who rescued them, "when they were 'cast out, pardon the pun' in someone's scrap-metal pile. I always have my men on my mind," Barbara jokes.

On this page, an old agate spittoon has been slipped over a garden perennial, and a fantasy scene created. Barbara anchored another little guy to a special veined stone she'd been saving. He now stands out among the drought-tolerant *Euphorbia myrsinites*. Another "handsome fellow" stands by a tree of spikes of yellow buttons that form wonderful seed pods.

On the facing page, an adopted "sad little dwarf hemlock" made an oasis for a happy pair in an old coal bucket. When Barbara found a shoe form in a nearby factory town, it seemed like the perfect perch for a footless fellow. Not long after that, she decided to utilize broken cinder blocks by filling them with the prescribed soil, sand, and stones for drainage, then planting them with foliage as well as with another man. Perhaps the luckiest figure is the man who cools

off in a two-by-four-foot water garden formed with leftover rubber roofing and lined with rocks from the woods. Another man has the wave of a politician. "That handsome man waves for your attention," she says. And probably Barbara waves back.

LEFT: Formerly used as a decorative element on the end of a rod that reinforced an old building, this star is now embedded in the walkway of an herb garden with a celestial theme. The darkly colored crushed limestone, with its flecks of white, represents the sky and stars. Iron stars are much sought after for their decorative possibilities. Look for them in antiques shops and flea markets.

RIGHT: English chimney pots, fired at high temperatures and often glazed, are being salvaged from old buildings to serve a new function as regal garden ornaments. This one sits bold and unadorned among herbs, its crown-like top adding to the overall attraction. Chimney pots with plainer tops are perfect places to settle pots of flowering plants and trailing vines.

BELOW: This once-neglected eyesore now a working outhouse is one gardener's contribution to keeping Americana alive. The structure was shingled in cedar, the windows were covered with decorative heat registers, and a floral motif was painted across the door. Then the top of this refurbished two-seater was turned into a roof garden planted with seasonal flowers.

ABOVE: When a local Greek restaurant tore down its back porch and needed someone to haul away the concrete columns, a gardener with a flair for history transported the remnants to her garden. There, she has playfully re-created the feeling of a ruined Acropolis, carpeting the ground with 23 varieties of fragrant thyme to reinforce the pun.

LEFT: Because "a Greek ruin is nothing without the head of a Greek god or goddess," a ceramist friend of the gardener supplied a flawed head of David that had been on its way to the studio's recycling bin.

LEFT: This antique fishing-net float has settled on dry land, its sea-green color harmonizing with the ivy surroundings.

RIGHT: An aqua-colored glass insulator, once part of a telephone pole installation, has become a light-reflecting garden object. It is complemented by the foliage of the calluna behind it and the silvery salvia in the foreground. Hard-to-find glass insulators have become collectible for their luminous color.

ABOVE: "Gossiping Stones" is what gardeners named their their arrangement of local rocks. They rise much like Stonehenge from their creeping phlox ground cover.

FOLLOWING PAGES: A bit of smart bartering was needed to acquire a weathered iron gate used to hold back boisterous Switzerland daisies, which bloom copiously throughout the summer until frost.

The Lucky Garden

The unique penny ball is "simple as pie," according to the garden owner who created her own version of an orb.

   The first step is to rob every purse and piggy bank of pennies. Then glue the pennies, heads up, onto an old bowling ball, which might be found at a local thriftshop or garage sale. After the durable outdoor glue dries, the next step is to grout it with a tinted, rust-colored mortar. Finally, a polyurethane sealant is brushed onto the ball and allowed to dry completely before the ball finds just the right spot in the garden. This lucky penny ball brings good fortune to a ground cover of *Acena chilonensis*.

Diminutive Objects

Pull aside a vine and Cupid says *hello*; walk through the rose garden and an angel catches your fancy; pause by a small lead bird and a real one will soon appear. Much like a pansy's elfin face, these small garden objects capture our attention and make us smile. Tucked into a garden's many nooks and crannies, they make grand statements. It's easy to change your mind and move these lightweight features to another container or another garden bed. This is especially appealing to gardeners who have a penchant for changing things around and will rearrange their outdoor decor on a whim. While some may moan, "Too much fuss!" others

will cry, "Oh, to find the perfect spot for just one more!"

Tiny objects often arrive in the form of garden gifts and souvenirs. "My garden is a treasure trove of gifts, thoughtful little tokens from people who appreciate the garden and the gardener,"

says someone who remembers each giver "on bended knee!"

COUNTRY INFLUENCES

When it comes to irrepressible appeal, the hands-down winners are the crafted objects that immediately suggest the heart of country. A barnyard pig cast in stone, a deer created from old metal tools, a humble hand plow are the inspiration, for their common theme is folk art and a nostalgia for rural living. In our gardens, we're not all that far removed from that fond remembrance.

RIGHT: Much of the fun of acquiring a new garden object is finding the perfect spot for it, a place that suits a particular flower bed or garden site without upsetting its natural beauty and balance. An element of humor figured into the placement of this concrete pig, who roots through the rosemary near the base of an aged tree.

Not many of us live on farms and ranches now, but even if the closest you've come to a barnyard animal is the children's petting zoo, chances are you still have a soft place for objects that celebrate earthy traditions.

If you like your ceramic pigs cute and small, you'll have no trouble finding one to decorate the herb garden. If your taste runs to artistic limited editions, there's a 300-pound concrete pig waiting to rummage among the blooms. Artisans and artists alike have turned every imaginable material into garden objects. And they've fashioned found objects into treasures in more abstracted country forms.

In addition to enlivening the space, these country objects play a useful role in filling in the blanks in the garden, creating a focus or inviting us to take a closer look at the primrose.

When we place country icons in our gardens, we elevate the humble horse plow to primitive object and preserve it as a legitimate form of garden folk art. There's something wonderfully sculptural about the twisty forks of an early hay mower, the plow blade's graceful curve, or even the rusty band of a wagon-wheel frame.

It's difficult to resist buying a country garden object even when it's not for sale. Al Granger, who with his wife runs Glasbern, a Pennsylvania country inn, attended a garden center auction and spotted a charming bird-motif sculpture in the landscaped garden there. "I had stumbled onto the perfect birthday gift for Beth. And it wasn't for sale. Being an impulsive buyer, I knew I had to have it." After some gentle prodding, the owner allowed the sculpture to be auctioned off and it was Al's. It was placed in the kitchen patio garden, where Beth walks daily to gather fresh flowers and herbs for the inn.

ABOVE: A tin scaredy-cat moves slightly with the wind tries hard to and act as a scarecrow.

LEFT: Tall grasses have become the natural habitat of a fanciful painted iron "Blue Heron" by the Pennsylvania artisan who goes by the name of Simple. The heron has been placed near a circular driveway, where visitors are exuberantly greeted by this heron and two others.

RIGHT: Utilizing discarded metal tools and pieces of farm implements prevalent in the barnyards and fields of New England, sculptor Bill Heise of Burlington, Vermont, has created "Leaping Gazelle," who appears to revel in the autumn colors.

LEFT: An early English rabbit design has been meticulously replicated in iron. In this hare, the owners say they found "a naturalistic creature that is not too adorable."

ABOVE: Displayed on a thick carpet of mulch consisting of pine needles and leaves, this antique lead rooster has lots of room to strut his stuff.

RIGHT: When garden designer Margaret Burnett received her Masters degree, her sister sent this fitting gift. "Jumping for joy is the constant occupation of my amphibian yard guardian," she relates. "It reminds me not only to wish upon a star, but to reach for them too. This yard ornament is always found hopping about my garden, always celebrating and gleeful, reminding me how wonderful it is to be remembered and to share." In this photograph, early red cabbage and summer broccoli are being inspired to grow.

FAR RIGHT: Watering cans that find a place here are the favored old friends that cannot be easily replaced.

LEFT: A folk artist in Seattle, Mike Zitka, created this whimsical beehive birdhouse. Its yellow paint brightens dull days and seasons without blooms.

RIGHT: The king of the jungle, cut from an oil drum and hand-hammered by a Haitian artist, lurks in a stand of the ornamental grass *Miscanthus* 'Variegatus'. The gardener has chosen to nestle her folk art among lamb's ears, Russian sage, artemisia, and New England aster. Behind the lion are delphiniums and branches of a greengage plum, all combining to make the perfect jungle setting.

FOLLOWING PAGES, LEFT: A primitive garden plow was a recent purchase at a farm tag sale. The garden owners plan to find a shade vine to wrap around the wood-and-iron structure. In spring, a circle of birch where the plow now sits is filled with hundreds of daffodils and grape hyacinths that soften the appearance of the old plow.

FOLLOWING PAGES, RIGHT: The owners of this fine dog set among three varieties of hosta, a Japanese painted fern, and variegated Solomon's seal believe that imitation is the highest form of flattery because several friends purchased similar stone dogs after admiring theirs.

ABOVE: The iron rim of a wagon wheel found in the woods becomes folk art. The gardeners plan to plant morning glories so that their vines will twine around the circle.

ABOVE: This wonderful wooden wheelbarrow is easy to move to different parts of the garden as a decorative reminder of timeless inventions. When it's filled with flowers in bloom, it becomes a planter on wheels.

ABOVE: Folk artist Mike Zitka has placed one of his signature carved and painted crows at the top of a trateur, a frame for climbing vines made from cedar poles. He chose scarlet runner bean for his trellis for the bright orange flowers in the summer and large bean pods in early fall. He says the garden trateur "creates interest even in winter, after the beans have gone."

LEFT: For garden owners Susan and Jerry Lauren, who found this rusty old plow at a country auction, its weathered look combined with sculptural simplicity represents the true meaning of country living. They chose to treat it more like a piece of minimalist folk art and so placed it, unadorned, on a grassy stretch of lawn with their red barn for a backdrop.

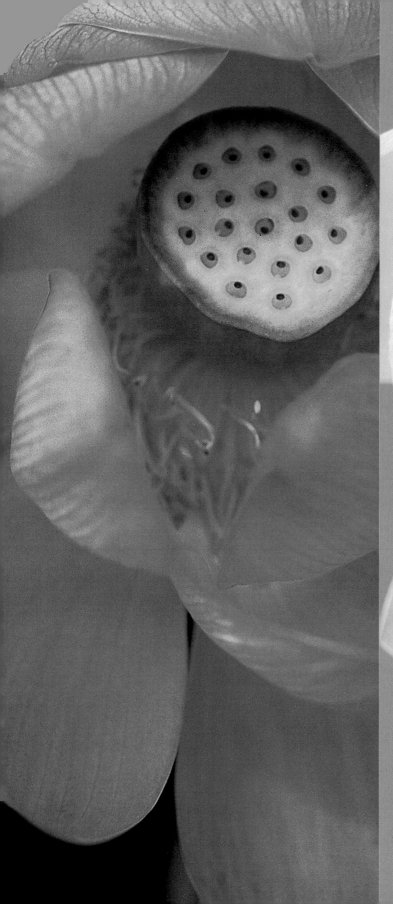

ARTFUL OBJECTS

A gallery as awesome as the great outdoors—that's exactly what gardener's create by placing fine art and artifacts in outdoor spaces. What better place for a large piece of sculpture than a rolling lawn with elbow room for giants? A cast stone Venus has genuine stage presence at the end of a graceful boxwood, and a carved Buddha in a mossy rock garden is art sharing the showcase with nature.

RIGHT: This bronze statue was acquired by Charles Mabon's grandfather during a trip through Italy early in this century. It was shipped to his Connecticut home where the fountain figure spit water into a pool, giving the arbor an air of tranquillity. Many years later, when "the estate was scattered to the wind," the sprite passed from view but not from memory. This cherished possession then played a final round of musical chairs, eventually finding a home with Charles and Ricky Mabon.

PRECEDING PAGES, LEFT: This vignette created around an avian piece is so naturalistic that, at first glance, one believes the iron dove's protective gesture toward her cracked stone egg is the real thing.

PRECEDING PAGES, RIGHT: "The African Lioness with Cubs," a bronze work by Georgia Gerber, assumes a convincingly vigilant stance in the feather grass. Not seen in this photograph are the two cubs she guards. After the sculpture was positioned, the plantings were designed around it.

LEFT: Carved from volcanic rock, this flute player from Costa Rica is surrounded by autumn leaves and a black walnut that has dropped from a nearby tree.

ABOVE: Because the gardener had visited India on a vacation, she holds a special fondness for this garden relic, a piece that would commonly be found on the ornate facades of Hindu temples. The purple smokebush adds a burst of color to the carved gray stonework.

LEFT: This Oriental sage sits on a great fish, a sign of bounty in the garden. The weathered cast iron blends well with the stone wall setting.

ABOVE: "Sky Lark" was created by the Portland, Oregon, artist Marty
Eichinger. A limited-edition sculpture made of cast bronze, the
goddess of air has been placed in the tree-lined courtyard garden,
where her blithe spirit is contagious.

ABOVE: A naturalistic sculpture designed by George Little and David Lewis has been skillfully cast in concrete and then color-washed. A contemporary example of the union between fine craft and fine art, it sits unobtrusively in a bed of real *Hosta sieboldiana* and clover-like osalis.

LEFT AND ABOVE: Arlene Wright and David Arntson of Seattle knew they wanted a showplace where they could do a great deal of entertaining, so they asked landscape design consultant R. David Adams to work with them. The floor of their spacious patio is rose-colored stone selected from a quarry in Flagstaff, Arizona. It provides a graceful, uninterrupted surface for their many grand-scale objects, contemporary works combined with antique pieces displayed in what can only be described as a glorious gallery-like setting. The distinguished lion is cast bronze. He was found in southern California at an antiques shop and is one of a pair.

LEFT: This enigmatic head was constructed of gray clay by northwestern artist Jena Glenn as a gift for her parents' garden. An old cement pot serves as the base. Sitting among wild ginger, the piece has been given a dash of color with a gladwyn iris seed pod.

RIGHT: As a tribute to their affection for New York City, a couple from the South commissioned metal artist Willy Ferguson to create the "Big Apple" for their garden. The rusty weathered finish of the iron sculpture stands out against the changing leaves of the red oak.

THE KINDNESS OF SAINT FRANCIS

A monarch butterfly may fail to appreciate the blessing of Saint Francis as it hovers briefly, then alights on his saintly stone head. And the local wrens could hardly care less about the architectural details of their postmodern birdhouse as they fuss about to make it home. Yet word tends to get around when a garden's been created with nature's creatures in mind.

LEFT: An apostle pot made from the casting of an ancient urn is the centerpiece of a circle that contains herbs related to Advent. The kindly figure of Saint Francis is especially well suited to this garden's biblical theme.

Birds and butterflies, as well as many animals and insects familiar to gardens, provide a venerable theme for decorative objects. The astounding variety of urns, statuary, plaques, feeders, and dwellings nurtures these native visitors in a beneficial way and, at the same time, humbly celebrates their presence through naturalistic designs.

Many gardeners say they look for wildlife images that make them smile, especially when they kneel to weed nearby. "It probably does more for me than it does for the animals," quips one gardener. "But I'm drawn like a magnet to objects with themes and sayings that symbolize the peace I feel when wild visitors are drawn to my garden." Artists and artisans from many countries certainly seem to feel the same way. They trans-

LEFT: David Halsaver, a gardener by vocation and an avocational carpenter, describes the vibrant blue bird shed he made for a garden on Bainbridge Island, Washington: "To make my structure appear striking yet still weathered, I used old barn wood and gave it three coats of paint, sanding down well between each layer. I was fortunate to have large sheets of thin copper that had been left outdoors for many years, creating a beautiful verdigris finish that I could never have hoped to duplicate. A large roof keeps the bird shed dry. The two chimney stacks are to fill the shed with birdseed. I wanted the birds to feel relaxed as they feed, so I placed it in a very secluded area thick with maples and rhododendron. All year long, it's Dinner is served!"

form clay into woodland dramas; sheet metal into dramatic sculptural forms imitating nature. Form and function unite. Such undiluted enthusiasm has even inspired a few gardeners to become self-trained carpenters as they learn to keep their green thumb out of harm's way.

Savvy gardeners learn to think like the wildlife they're courting. They'll attract more visitors where butterfly bush and rosemary grow. They save the bird feeder for a shaded ivy trellis, setting it high enough to keep furry friends at bay and sheltered enough to keep seeds dry. They tuck them among dense plantings, near an area redolent with honeysuckle blossoms, in a rugged rock environment to ensure a bit of privacy. As for the decorative motifs the animals may not notice. But why take the chance?

Dale Meyers, who enjoys as much of his retirement as possible outdoors in his Virginia garden, unearthed a stone frog concealed by a

ABOVE: A gardener who never tires of new objects, swaps garden ornamentation with her father, also an avid gardener living just two blocks away. This patriotic birdhouse is one of the more coveted swaps, especially on the Fourth of July.

thick growth of ivy when excavating a 45-year-old garden. "The frog was buried in a small pond," he told me. The bricks and the stones of the original pond were recycled, and the worn and mossy old bullfrog was placed on a large boulder overlooking the pond and fountain. Birds, squirrels, butterflies, and other small animals now come to rest and refresh at the pond, sharing the filtered shade and animating the stone frog by their presence.

There's a frenzied crew of hummingbirds who dive-bomb from the big lilac bush to the feeder hung near the porch at our farmhouse. We swear they get noticeably piqued when we fail to refill the feeder. Perhaps this simple plastic feeder with its rosy homemade nectar is our most treasured garden object for its entertainment value alone. Our frustrated cats, who are constantly outmaneuvered by the little humdingers, might not agree.

ABOVE: A hanging birdhouse is effective in filling the space between the
windows of Douglas Martin's stucco-style cottage in Richmond, Virginia,
colorfully accented by flowers in a planter hung just below it.

RIGHT: The soft muted colors of a well-seasoned birdhouse blend well
with the herbs' gray and silver foliage.

RIGHT: Since purple martins are beneficial for organic gardeners, consuming as they do many insects harmful to plants and flowers, Terri Hevener decided to make this roomy martin house a focal point in her Monterey, Virginia, backyard garden. "We haven't had any colonies yet," she says, "but each spring we put out a vacancy sign!"

FOLLOWING PAGES, LEFT: Hoping to attract the local mourning dove population, Eve and Per Thyrum found inspiration for their birdhouse in designs of dovecotes seen in England and Scotland. When Per acquired an antique copper roof at an estate sale, it seemed the perfect beginning for this splendid eight-compartment house, which seems to have taken on a distinctly Oriental grace. The individual compartments are serviceable by doors on either side. The structure is supported by pressure-treated posts that have been stained dark to blend with the upper part.

FOLLOWING PAGES, RIGHT: Bee skeps have a symbolic role in today's herb gardens, serving as a remembrance of skeps that date back to the eighteenth century, when they were kept to attract bees that would pollinate plants and provide a source of honey.

ABOVE: A simple bluebird house, made to bluebird-specific dimensions, sits on the picketed perimeter of the yard, where the garden becomes wilder and bolder with a romp of *Petasites japonicus*.

ABOVE: In the very same garden, another plain birdhouse, perched on
a tall iron rod, is a welcome refuge in a secluded corner of the
garden. Some gardeners say they are more concerned with
providing shelter than with making an architectural statement.

LEFT: The birds may not notice, but the people who purchased this neoclassic birdhouse enjoy its splendid white design towering above their lush summer garden, where birds can enjoy the privacy of their natural surroundings and perhaps appreciate the fine design of their house.

LEFT: Upon seeing this photograph, Barbara Gornto, a keen observer of how light affects garden objects, said of her bas-relief bird feeder, "This is the way I would like the shadows to look all the time." Hand cast in bonded marble and given a patina finish, the feeder has been mounted on the front wall of a Japanese-style garden so that the owner can see it from inside the house, giving her a pleasant indoor place in which to meditate and commune with nature.

RIGHT: A rustic birdhouse that doubles as a feeder is sheltered by the vines of the arbor, providing shade and seclusion.

ABOVE: Although they were designed to be used as small fountains, these cheerful ceramic sunflowers do nicely as wall feeders until the owners can incorporate the piping of water into their garden plans.

LEFT: Several ordinary bird feeders draw attention as they catch the golden glow of a late summer afternoon. The owners are pleased with the graceful lines of the wrought-iron feeder stand, which raises the functional feeders a notch above the competition.

LEFT: This bird-feeder garden marker is set amid golden barberry, which develops red berries in the autumn and attracts even more birds. Marveen and Michael Pakalik fill this one with water, pointing out that seeds would disperse in a garden bed and make weeding even more onerous.

RIGHT: If a love of gardening is an inborn trait, then Nancy Woodard inherited her mother's love of gardening as well as a few treasured garden possessions. This charming bird feeder was one of the things Nancy's mother chose to take along when she moved from a large home to a more manageable apartment with a courtyard, where ever-faithful birds continued to visit until the end of her life. This small object has been the source of pleasure for two generations, as well as a symbolic tie of affection.

A Small Housing Development

Several spanking-new birdhouses, like the one shown here, were constructed and painted by students from Coyote Junior High School in Seattle, Washington, who participated in a summertime Hit the Streets project. Not only did they help develop a local pocket park, they also made handcrafted objects to finish the space.

Mary Beth Satterlee, the Coyote Junior High School director, recommends that beginners concentrate more on basic construction than on getting too fancy. The students began by making a pattern for their birdhouse on brown paper and stenciling the pattern onto sheets of plywood. After the pieces were cut and assembled with wood glue and tacks, they applied ordinary house paint. Although the bright colors will weather over time, leftover paint is great for later touch-ups. Use a coat of exterior varnish for additional weatherproofing.

These birdhouses are waiting for installation on 15-foot poles decorated just as brightly as the houses.

ABOVE: Garden owners made this birdcage to hold a nasty parrot who attacked everyone within reach and was eventually returned to the pet store. The parrot was replaced by doves, "as a symbol of love and peace in our home." The tranquil birds spend their days in the courtyard garden.

LEFT: Since this portable ceramic water garden reflects something primal and woodsy, the owner perched it on a rock wall in a shade garden near a hollowed-out tree trunk and the very soft and flowing grass *Hakonechloa* 'Aureola.' Sitting in the center of the scene is *Acorus gramineus minima* and a floating duckweed. Whenever a centerpiece is needed inside the house, the entire water garden, made by Swamp Fox in Chadds Ford, Pennsylvania, is picked up and moved inside.

A GARDEN
DIVIDED

A familiar garden gate bids us welcome; a picket fence, neat and orderly, frames our space; a rugged stone wall unifies; steppingstones connect. These elements establish a garden's unique boundaries, some tangible and others related to the soul, and make a piece of earth a gardener's own. These vital dividers have more than one mission: While offering their own form of decorative expression, they enhance the space by blending in with the various garden objects on the property.

LEFT: Antique English iron "hoops" in the shape of branches reinforce the edges of this garden.

ABOVE: A massive iron cauldron with plantings provides additional form and height as it breaks up the space between a low rock wall and the rail fencing in the distance.

LEFT: Birdhouses are ubiquitous, attesting to Americans' age-old love affair with the wildlife within their private spaces. Exceptional birdhouses that we can date to an earlier day with some degree of certainty are more difficult to find. This diminutive vintage replica of a rustic dwelling shows an admirable attention to detail in the dormer windows as well as the long porch across the front, which is supported by posts. The real story is lost to an anonymous homespun history, but the new owners are happy to ponder their charming dwelling's origins.

For Mother Margaret

Connecticut garden designer Margaret Burnett woke up on Mother's Day morning, 1997, to discover a special surprise: a garden post displayed at the corner of the vegetable garden within easy view of the kitchen window. The post was made by Carly, Margaret's 12-year-old stepdaughter, and decorated with "a botanically correct canary bird vine."

The construction methods Carly's father used to produce Mother Margaret's garden post involved rehabilitating a discarded hollow newel post by scrubbing, sanding, and then painting. A rot-resistant pole—cedar or pressure-treated—sized to fit inside the shell of the hollow newel post was driven partway into a hole in the ground, dug at the selected site. The soil was then packed firmly around the pole. The newel post was then slipped over the pole and secured with a brass screw on each side. Carly decorated the post in secret so the surprise was complete at the time of installation.

ABOVE: Handcrafted pottery with a southwestern motif adds interest to this stone wall. Many gardeners give their pots needed stability on windy days by filling them with heavy stones.

LEFT: Rustic fencing and stonework, with a bright flourish of plantings, divide the upper part of this garden from the bog garden now hidden behind it.

ABOVE: An enormous iron tub blooms with bright geraniums and *Ajuga* at the entrance of a driveway that follows an old stone wall. It tells guests new to the area just where to turn in and greets them with its brightness all summer long.

ABOVE: The stones were taken, one by one, from the earth as three large garden borders evolved behind the house. This wall was built free-form, from those stones. Unfortunately, it is constantly in need of repair as deer knock it over. A variety of day lilies was planted to fill in and mask the foliage of the many daffodils and narcissus, which frame the stone wall in the spring with their exuberant blooming.

LEFT: Say "picket fence" and you conjure up visions of Tom Sawyer's foolery and Mr. McGregor's forbidden garden. Although there are dozens upon dozens of picket fence designs, most gardeners opt for the pleasant basic pickets, posts, and stringers. This traditional picket fence, left in its natural wood state, has begun to weather. It contains an ambitious vegetable garden and delineates the space.

LEFT AND RIGHT: When the strong straight lines of their arbor needed curves and texture, inventive garden owners located a wrought-iron fence in a salvage yard, the original red paint of which had weathered in an interesting way. With just a bit of work, they were able to install the fencing along the arbor's open spaces to make it look as though the ornamental fence had been there forever.

ABOVE: A natural "fence" is created by using pliable twigs and lacing them together with rope or leather in a trellis design to hold up top-heavy blossoms, such as this *Tradescantia*. The good thing about this rustic fence is that anyone can make it look authentic.

ABOVE: A gardener who has an objection to modern hose keepers on aesthetic grounds has driven a large old spike into the earth for the usually unmanageable hose line.

Following pages, left: A wide-arched trellis holds roses and hydrangeas and dramatically, establishes the opening to a smaller garden beyond.

Following pages, right: Part of an old trellis was anchored where tall plants and determined vines might find a tall place to climb.

LEFT: Most gardeners appreciate the beauty and function of a garden support by any name. Among the many possibilities: tower, obelisk, vine trainer (*trateur* or *treillage* in French); or, quite simply, a standard form upon which flowers and vines can meander. Whatever you choose to call it, this ancient form has been relied upon by gardeners since the time of Augustus Caesar.

RIGHT: The large urn seen in the distance, a reproduction of a pot used to store olives, weathers well. Used as the focal point in the arbor, the terra-cotta pot was imported from Italy.

FOLLOWING PAGES, LEFT: A wrought-iron obelisk adds interest to a tiny luxuriant English-style garden barely a step from the sidewalk. The eerie light only moments before a tempestuous thunderstorm highlights the predominant plants, including Mexican daisy, several types of asters, black snakeroot, and purple jewel berry.

FOLLOWING PAGES, RIGHT: A bridge of concrete tiles, the reveal filled with soil, depicts nature's elements. It spans a short stretch from the driveway to the garden beyond.

WITH THANKS

GARDENING IS AN EXERCISE IN OPTIMISM. SOMETIMES, IT IS THE
TRIUMPH OF HOPE OVER EXPERIENCE. —*Marina Schinz, 1985*

The old friends and new acquaintances whose gardens appear in *Decorating Your Garden* wasted no time in taking me under their wings. Going well beyond basic hospitality, they offered me free run of their lovely gardens, cold lemonade on sweltering days, a pleasant guest room, and, always, their good company. When the time came, they completed my lengthy questionnaire and added pages of notes filled with engaging anecdotes and indispensable information. In turn, I tried hard not to flatten their flower beds with my tripod or litter their lawns with empty film canisters.

I began this project in Virginia and am especially grateful to Margaret Ray and to the Virginia Beach gardeners: Ann Callis, Barbara Gornto, Dale and Jan Meyers, Millie Rutter, Audrey Wilson, Karen and Pope Woodard, Nancy and Jimmy Woodard; and also to Douglas Martin from Richmond.

Moving on to the western part of the state, many thanks to Don Haynie and Tom Hamlin, whose renowned Buffalo Springs Herb Farm is also their home, Elizabeth and Bruce Campbell and their daughter Katherine, and Tommie and Bob Duke, whose challenging garden project inspired Tommie to open Duke & Penn, a garden shop in Staunton, Virginia, with her brother, Stephen Fitzpenn. Thanks are also due to Terri Hevener, whose town garden is right behind her charming shop, The Personal Touch, in Monterey. Other Virginia support came from Rusty Lilly, Doug and Tidge Roller, Mary Ann Foster, Charlotte Frishkorn, and Betsy Little.

Midsummer found me in northwest Connecticut with Evan Hughes and Peter Ermacora, whose friendship network is always amazing. The contingent in that area includes: Margaret Burnett, whose garden mishap turned into valuable time together, Fred and Marcie Imberman, Susan and Jerry Lauren, Charles and Ricky Mabon, Suzanne and Ted Marolda, Alison Fox, and Marveen and Michael Pakalik.

In the Seattle area, the boundless garden talent included: Linda Cochran, Brian Coleman, Diane Glenn, Elana Korakianitou Pors, Mary Beth and Jerry Satterlee, Ingrid and Stanley Savage, Karla and

Gary Waterman, Mike Zitka, Arlene Wright, and David Arnston. Since the Bainbridge Island, Washington, home garden of George Little and David Lewis is also a showcase for their own garden sculpture business, Little & Lewis, it was exciting to admire objects that I could actually order on the spot. Their special work, while not always identified in captions, appears on the following pages: 20, 24 (above), 27, 28, 29 (right), 61, 87, 98, 118, 119, 181, and 237. The northwest connection was further made possible by Geri Williams, who made sure I wasn't sleepless in Seattle, Andrea Hamilton, Kari Morgan, who kept me sane in the rain, Joan Loop, Betty Balcolm, R. David Adams, Andy Looney, and Gillian Matthews at Ravenna Gardens.

In Pennsylvania, Delaware, and New York, a smaller yet still valiant group of garden owners welcomed me: Al and Beth Granger, Barbara Pressler, Joni Nelson, Eve and Per Thyrum, and Betty Sherrill, whose daffodils are legendary. Always on the sidelines were Charles Muise, Gene Heil, Marsha Schmidt, Joan Lesser, Erika and Gary Matt, and Dylan Landis.

During the course of this project, Jose Gaytan offered frequent technical advice, Marc Berenson came through with fine film editing during a frenzied time, and Ellen Spector Platt thoughtfully photographed the whimsical outhouse on page 134. The fine staff at Time-Life Books extended their constant support and enthusiasm for this project, especially Kate Hartson, with her creative eye and good instincts; Jennifer Lee, a true renaissance woman; art director Christopher Register, who provided essential deftness; Liz Ziehl, Donia Steele, and Olga Vezeris. It was good to have Barbara Clark back for the words and the logic. Howard Klein, the book's designer, took the fine art of design above and beyond the norm with an exquisite presentation that perfectly captures the spirit of this book and my hopes for what it would eventually look like.

Unfortunately, garden owners didn't always know the names or the locations of many artists and artisans whose work appears throughout *Decorating Your Garden*. I apologize when our research failed to track them down. I wish to thank the ones I did find for allowing me to photograph their work: Betz Bernhard, Marty Eichinger, Willy Ferguson, Georgia Gerber, William Heise, and L'Deane Trueblood.

As a photographer and as a person, my loving partner, Ken McGraw, possesses the gentle patience that I lack. I thank him for his special shots of butterflies and birds that appear in this book as well as for the water snake picture that I refused to include.